Why Why Why do clocks have hands?

Miles Kelly

PUBLISHING

First published in 2007 by
Miles Kelly Publishing Ltd
Bardfield Centre, Great Bardfield, Essex, CM7 4SL

Copyright © Miles Kelly Publishing Ltd 2007

2 4 6 8 10 9 7 5 3 1

Editorial Director
Belinda Gallagher

Art Director
Jo Brewer

Assistant Editor
Lucy Dowling

Volume Designer
Sally Lace

Indexer
Hilary Bird

Production Manager
Elizabeth Brunwin

Reprographics
Anthony Cambray, Liberty Newton, Ian Paulyn

ISBN 978-1-84236-908-1

Printed in China

British Library Cataloguing-in-Publication Data
A catalogue record for this book is available
from the British Library

www.mileskelly.net
info@mileskelly.net

Contents

What were the first inventions?

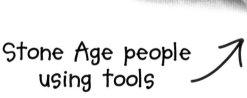

 **The first inventions were stone tools, which early people began to make about two million years ago.** During the Stone Age, about 30,000 years ago, people discovered how to sew animal skins together to make clothes. They also learnt how to keep warm and dry by building shelters.

Stone Age people using tools ↗

How did early people see in the dark?

Prehistoric people used lamps to light up caves. The lamps were made of clay or stone saucers, which were filled with animal fat. The animal fat was then burnt using a wick made of moss.

Fire-makers!

Early people discovered how to make fire more than 250,000 years ago! Thousands of years later, flint stones were used to make sparks, which lit dried grass and wood.

Who invented the wheel?

The Sumerian people invented wheels 5500 years ago. They were heavy and made with carved wood that was fastened together. Later, the ancient Egyptians made spoked wheels, which were lighter.

Count

In this book, how many inventions can you find that use the wheel?

Spoked wheels

Who invented the first car?

Karl Benz invented the first car in 1896. It had a petrol-powered engine but could not travel very fast. The first popular car was the Model T, built in 1908 by the Ford company in the United States. Over 15 million of them were sold worldwide.

Model T Ford

Why do tractors have such big tyres?

Tractors were invented in 1892 and are used to pull farm machinery, such as ploughs. Tractors have huge tyres to stop them getting stuck in mud. Big weights at the front stop tractors tipping over when pulling heavy machinery.

Tractor

Wooden lines!

Railway tracks were once made of wood! Wheels move more easily along rails, so horses pulled wagons on wooden rails more than 400 years ago. Metal rails were invented in 1789.

What was a boneshaker?

A boneshaker was one of the first bicycles. It had solid tyres and was so uncomfortable to ride that it made people's bones shake. In 1888, John Dunlop invented air-filled rubber tyres that made cycling more comfortable.

Try

If you have a bike, try riding it in the garden. Is it a smooth or bumpy ride?

Who used the first sails?

Sails were invented by the Egyptians more than 5000 years ago. About 2000 years ago, the best sailors were the Phoenician people. They sailed in boats made of cedar wood and reeds. These ships had sails and oars and were used to make long journeys.

Draw

Using coloured pens or pencils, draw your own super sail boat. Try adding your own amazing inventions.

Phoenician boat

Why did coal miners need steam power?

Before steam power, miners had to pull coal carts out of mines by hand. This was very hard work. Then in 1814, a coal miner named George Stephenson invented an engine that pulled the carts out of the mines using steam power.

Maglev train

Can trains float?

Yes they can, in a way. In 1909 Robert Goddard discovered a way to make trains travel using magnets. These trains are called Maglevs. They run on a magnetic rail that pushes the train up so it seems to be floating. Maglevs can reach very high speeds.

9

What is a combine harvester?

A combine harvester is a big farm machine that cuts crops and separates grain. The first combine harvester was invented in 1836 and was pulled by horses. Today, farmers all over the world use these machines so they can harvest their crops quickly.

Combine harvester

Plant power!

Scientists are changing the way plants grow. They have invented ways of creating crops with built-in protection from pests and diseases.

Can ships fly?

Airships can! They are filled with a special gas called helium. This gas is lighter than air, and makes the airship float in the sky. Today, airships are used to display adverts in the sky and are not used for people to travel in.

Airship

Did people pull ploughs?

Ploughs were invented in Egypt around 2000 BC and were first pulled by people. They helped farmers break up the ground and turn the soil over. Later, people began to use horses and oxen to pull ploughs.

Think

Can you think of any other machines or animals that you would find on a farm?

Who invented jumbo jets?

A jumbo jet is a plane. In 1970, the first jumbo jet flight took place between New York and London. The planes are powered by jet engines that were invented by Dr Hans von Ohain of Germany, and Sir Frank Whittle of England. Their inventions developed to become modern jet engines.

Jumbo jet

Bird brains!

Many inventors have tried to fly by flapping birdlike wings. All have failed. One of the first bird-men crashed to his death at a Roman festival in the 1st century AD.

Can balloons carry people?

Hot-air balloons were invented in 1783. They can carry people high up into the sky. The first ever passengers to fly in a hot air balloon were not humans but a cockeral, a duck and a sheep!

Do planes perform tricks?

Yes, they do. The Red Arrows are a team of highly skilled pilots that can make their planes perform tricks. Their red aircrafts can fly upside down and on their sides and are very fast. The Red Arrows perform in front of large crowds at airshows and other special occasions.

Make

With some paper, make a plane and colour it in. How far can you get it to fly?

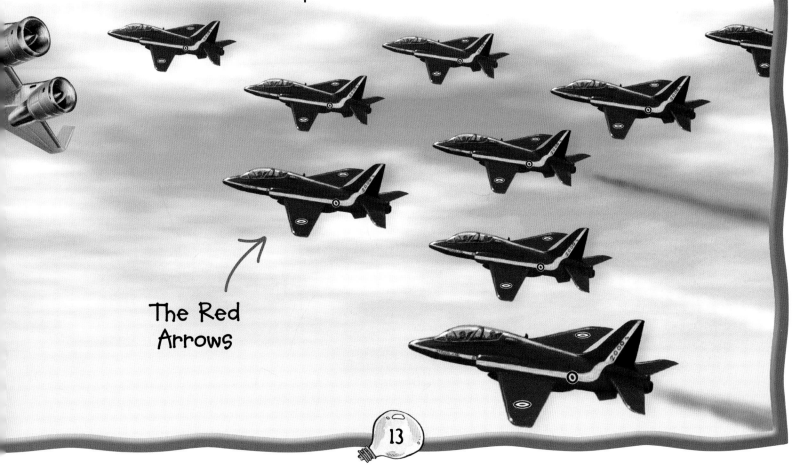

The Red Arrows

How can we see into space?

People can look at the stars and planets by using a telescope. The first telescope was invented by a Dutchman called Hans Lippershey in 1608. In 1609, the Italian scientist Galileo built his own telescope. He was the first person to see the craters on the Moon.

Telescope

Who invented spectacles?

The Italians did. In the 14th century in Italy people made their own glass lenses to look through. These small lenses were put into frames and were used to help people to read.

Write

Imagine you have found a pair of magic spectacles. Write a story about what you see when you put them on.

Microscope

How can we make small things bigger?

By using a microscope. A microscope uses pieces of glass called lenses. These make small things look bigger than they really are. The first microscope was invented in the 1600s and had one lens. Later microscopes had two lenses to make them more powerful.

Marvellous maths!

Around AD 300, the Chinese invented a counting machine called an abacus. It was a wooden frame with beads strung on wires and it helped people do complicated sums.

Who made the streets light up?

Street lamp

An Austrian named Carl Auer did, in the late 1800s. He invented a lamp called a gas mantle that glowed very brightly when heated up. The gas mantle was used in the first street lamps. Long torches were needed to light the lamps.

Wind power!

The first windmills were invented thousands of years ago. They helped to grind grain into flour. Today, windmills are used to pump water, make electricity and power machinery.

How big was the first computer?

The first computer was so big that it took up a whole room. In 1975, the first home computers were made but they were expensive and not very powerful. Computers today are small, cheap and powerful.

Wind turbine

Who made electricity from the wind?

In 1888, Charles F Brush invented a modern-day windmill called a wind turbine. Wind turbines have blades that turn in the wind. These power a motor inside the turbine, which makes electricity. Wind turbines can power entire towns.

Remember

In ancient times, what was the name of the counting machine that was invented by the Chinese?

Why do clocks have hands?

Clocks have hands so that people can tell the time. The hands point to different numbers on the clock face and these tell us what time it is. Clocks work by using a series of springs and wheels that move the hands of the clock around. The first mechanical alarm clock was invented in 1787.

Make

Use a paper plate to make a clock. Write the numbers on the face and use plastic straws for the hands.

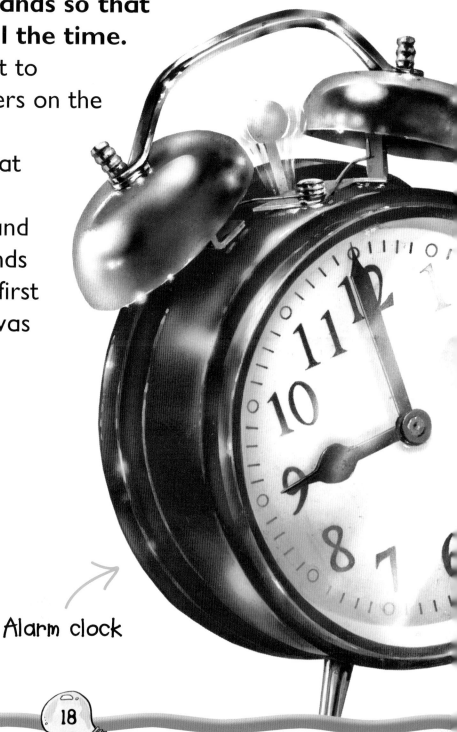

Alarm clock

How does the Sun tell the time?

The Sun was used to help people tell the time before clocks were invented. Sundials have a stone face marked with the hours, and a pointer that makes a shadow when the Sun is shining on it. Whatever hour the shadow falls on is the time at that moment.

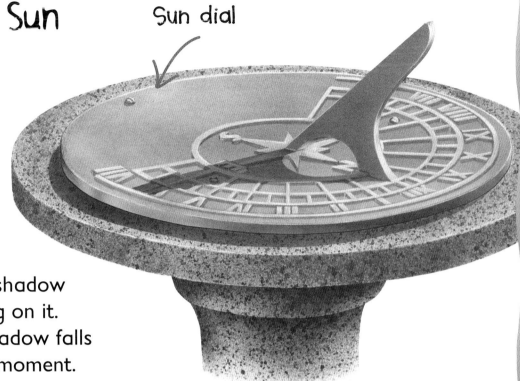
Sun dial

Watch it!

The wrist watch was invented in the 1600s by a French mathematician. He attached a piece of string to his pocket watch and tied it around his wrist.

Can candles tell the time?

Candles were once used as clocks to tell the time. They were marked with rings so that when the wax burnt down, people could tell how much time has passed by.

When was cooking invented?

Cooking was invented in prehistoric times by some of our earliest relatives. When people discovered fire, they realized that if food was placed in the fire, it tasted better. Cooking also made food safer because it killed germs that might cause sickness.

The first cooks

Who wrote the first words?

The Sumerian people wrote the first words more than 5500 years ago. They scratched words onto clay tablets. The first writing was made up of pictures. Ancient picture-writing used hundreds of different signs. Today, modern alphabets have far fewer letters.

Write

Using pictures instead of words, write a secret message. Can your friends work out what it says?

Alexander Graham Bell

Smoky signals!

Before inventions such as the telephone, sending long-distance messages had to be simple. Native Americans used smoke signals to send messages to each other.

Who made the first phone call?

Alexander Graham Bell made the first telephone call in 1876. The telephone worked by turning vibrations in the human voice into electrical signals. These signals travelled down a wire to another phone, where they were turned back into sound.

What was a gramophone?

In 1887, Emile Berlin invented a machine that could play music. The machine was called a gramophone. To make it work, a handle was turned, which turned a disk under a steel needle. The needle allowed the music to play.

Gramophone

Find out
Today we use CDs to play music. Can you find out what the letters CD are short for?

Marvellous movies!

Only one person at a time could watch the very first films. The viewer went into a special room and looked through a hole in a box.

Who invented television?

John Logie Baird invented the first television in 1926. The pictures were black and white and very blurry. Modern televisions show clear, sharp pictures in colour.

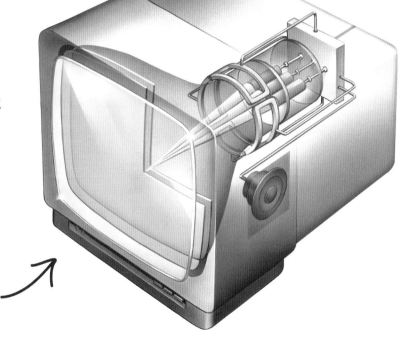

Television →

Who took the first photo?

Joseph Nicephore took the first-ever photograph in 1826. The picture was of rooftops and took eight hours to take. The first cameras were very big, and instead of paper, the photos were printed on glass plates.

Why were fridges dangerous?

The first electric refrigerators were invented in 1805, but they were dangerous to use. This was because they used a poisonous gas to keep them cold. In 1929, a safer gas called freon was used. However freon causes damage to the planet, so scientists want to change this, too.

Stone cold!

Stone Age people invented the first refrigerators! They buried any spare food in pits dug in ground that was always frozen.

Early fridge

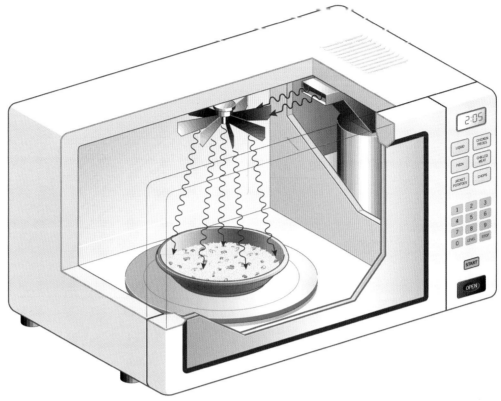

Microwave oven

How do microwaves cook food?

A microwave oven produces waves that make food heat itself up. In 1945, Percy L. Spencer invented the microwave oven after noticing that a microwave machine at his workplace had melted a chocolate bar in his pocket.

Look

Take a look around your house. How many inventions help you and your family every day?

Have toilets always flushed?

4000 years ago in Greece, royal palaces had flushing toilets that used rainwater. Thomas Twyford invented the first ceramic flushing toilet in 1885. His design is still used today.

What is special about the shuttle?

The space shuttle is a very special spacecraft. This is because it is reusable. Most spacecraft can only go into space once, but the shuttle is like a space plane. It can return into space up to ten times. The first space shuttle was launched in 1981.

Space shuttle →

Who invented fireworks?

The Chinese invented fireworks thousands of years ago. The loud sound that they made was supposed to frighten off evil spirits. Today, fireworks are used to celebrate special occasions.

Write

Imagine you are living on board a space station. Write a letter to tell people about your adventure.

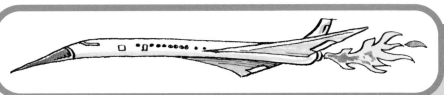

Fast flyer!

Concorde was a superfast plane that flew people across the Atlantic in record time. Trips from London to New York only took three hours.

Space station

Can people live in space?

Yes, they can. A space station is a home in space for astronauts. It has a kitchen for making meals, and cabins with sleeping bags. The first space station was launched in 1971.

Do zips have teeth?

Yes, zips do have teeth! A zip has two rows of teeth that can be opened and shut by a slider. The first zip was invented in 1891. It was called the Talon Slide Fastener and was used on a boot called the zipper. This is where the zip got its name from.

Zip →

Bone brush!

The first toothbrush was made out of animal bone. The bone had small holes drilled into it where bristles were placed.

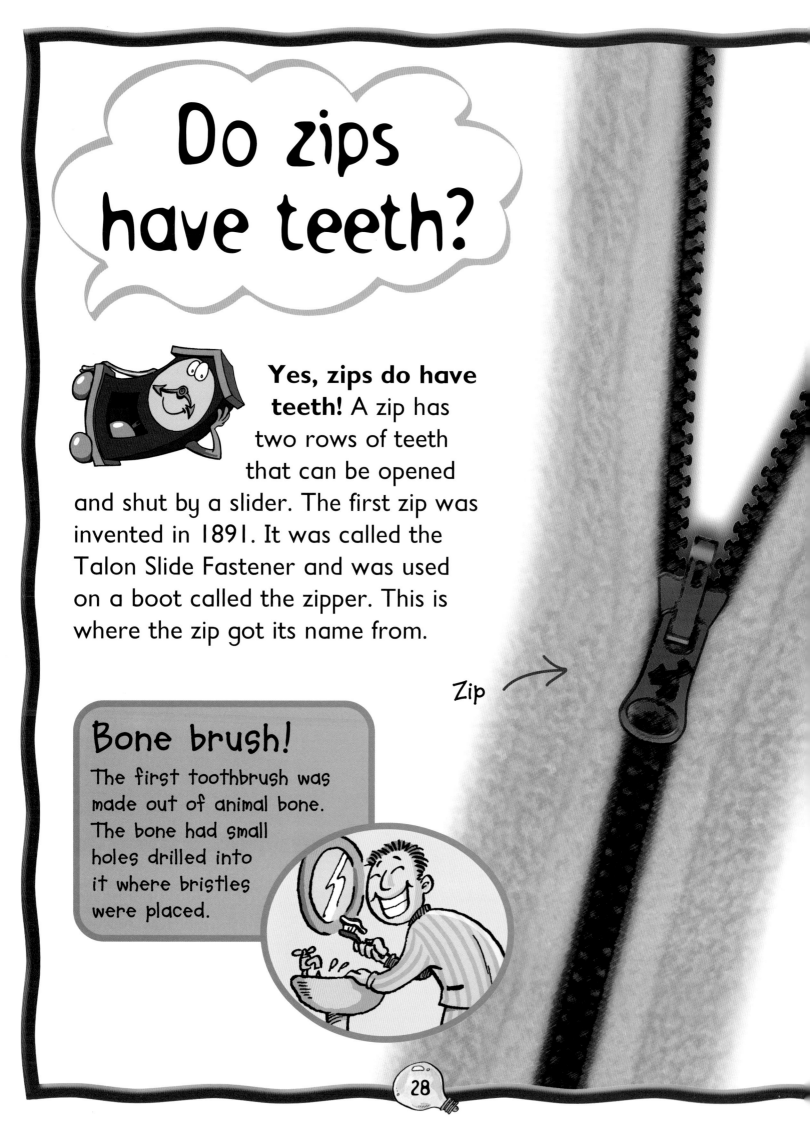

How did teddy bears get their name?

The teddy bear was named after US President Theodore Roosevelt in 1903. The president's nickname was Teddy. One day he spared the life of a bear cub when out hunting. The teddy bear became the most popular soft toy ever.

Which horse can rock?

The rocking horse was invented in 1780. It was a toy horse that children could ride on without hurting themselves. Early rocking horses were usually dapple-grey in colour and rocked on wooden bow rockers.

Draw

Design your own perfect toy. Draw a picture of it and colour it in.

Rocking horse

Quiz time

Do you remember what you have read about inventions? These questions will test your memory. The pictures will help you. If you get stuck, read the pages again.

3. What was a boneshaker?

page 7

4. Can trains float?

page 9

page 4

1. How did early people see in the dark?

5. Did people pull ploughs?

page 11

page 5

2. Who invented the wheel?

6. Can ships fly?

page 11

7. Who invented jumbo jets?

page 23

page 12

11. Who took the first photo?

8. Who invented spectacles?

page 26

page 15

12. What is special about the shuttle?

9. How does the Sun tell the time?

page 27

13. Who invented fireworks?

page 19

Answers

1. They used lamps made of clay and animal fat
2. The Sumerian people
3. One of the very first bicycles
4. Yes, the Maglev train can
5. Yes, the first ploughs were pulled by people
6. Airships can fly
7. Dr Hans von Ohain
8. The Italians
9. With a sundial
10. The Sumerian people
11. Joseph Nicephore
12. It can be reused
13. The Chinese

10. Who wrote the first words?

page 21

Index